CIVIC VALUES

RESPECT FOR RULES AND LAWS

ELIZABETH SCHULZ

Cavendish Square

New York

Published in 2018 by Cavendish Square Publishing, LLC
243 5th Avenue, Suite 136, New York, NY 10016

Website: cavendishsq.com

This publication represents the opinions and views of the author based on his or her personal
experience, knowledge, and research. The information in this book serves as a general guide
only. The author and publisher have used their best efforts in preparing this book and disclaim
liability rising directly or indirectly from the use and application of this book.

All websites were available and accurate when this book was sent to press.

Library of Congress Cataloging-in-Publication Data

Names: Schulz, Elizabeth, (Writer), author.
Title: Respect for rules and laws / Elizabeth Schulz.
Description: New York : Cavendish Square Publishing, 2018. | Series: Civic values | Includes index.
Identifiers: LCCN 2017025801 (print) | LCCN 2017026489 (ebook) | ISBN 9781502632074 (E-book) |
ISBN 9781502632043 (pbk.) | ISBN 9781502632050 (6 pack) | ISBN 9781502632067 (library bound)
Subjects: LCSH: Law--Juvenile literature. | Social norms--Juvenile literature.
Classification: LCC K240 (ebook) | LCC K240 .S38 2018 (print) | DDC 340/.115--dc23
LC record available at https://lccn.loc.gov/2017025801

Editorial Director: David McNamara
Editor: Kristen Susienka
Copy Editor: Rebecca Rohan
Associate Art Director: Amy Greenan
Designer: Alan Sliwinski
Production Coordinator: Karol Szymczuk
Photo Research: J8 Media

The photographs in this book are used by permission and through the courtesy of: Front cover, Kali9/istockphoto.
com; Back cover and throughout the book, Arosoft/Shutterstock.com; p. 4 James Weston/Shutterstock.com; p 6 CM
Dixon/Print Collector/Getty Images; pp. 7, 20 North Wind Picture Archives; p. 8 Casey Martin/Shutterstock.com; p.
9 Sakhorn/Shutterstock.com; p. 10 Zev Radovan/Bridgeman Images; p. 12 Dirck Halstead/Liaison/Hulton Archive/
Getty Images; p. 13 Unknown author/staff.4j.lane.edu/File: Twelve Tables Engraving.jpg/Wikimedia Commons;
pp. 15, 26 Everett Historical/Shutterstock.com; p. 16 Charles Haire/Shutterstock.com; p. 18 Stock Montage/Getty
Images; p. 21 Festa/Shutterstock.com; p. 24 Burlingham/Shutterstock.com; p. 27 Jim Pruitt/Shutterstock.com.

Printed in the United States of America

CONTENTS

Classroom Golden Rules

✓ We listen
✓ We are kind to others
✓ We always look after each other

Rules teach us how to behave and live with each other.

CHAPTER ONE

WHAT ARE RULES AND LAWS?

People around the world live together. They make communities. They make **societies**. Each person in a society helps one another. In a society, there are rules that state how people should behave. These rules are called civic values. All people in a society share civic values. Civic values are thoughts or actions that a society considers important. Examples of civic values are honesty and respect.

WHAT IS THE LAW?

The law is a system of rules. These rules help keep people happy and safe. Laws exist so people treat each other with respect. The earliest example of the law is found in ancient Egypt. The Egyptians had *Ma'at*. This was an idea that meant truth, balance, **order**, harmony, law, morality, and justice.

Other rules and laws protect civic values. But where do these rules and laws come from? How do people know to follow them?

Ancient Greeks and Romans were some of the first people to think of rules, laws, and rights. In ancient

Greece, they started a "civil society." Everyone in a civil society obeyed the rules and laws the Greeks thought were important. The ancient Romans were influenced by the Greeks. They studied laws. Laws told people the rules of their society, and laws also protected citizens.

Ancient Greeks shared ideas that became important to their society.

Civic Values, Rights, and Laws

Today, every society in the world has their own civic values and citizens' rights. "Rights" are protected under the **rule of law**. In the United States, American citizens have rights like the freedom of speech,

Breaking rules can sometimes send a citizen to jail.

freedom of religion, and freedom of the press. Not every country has the same rights. Some rights in one country are not rights in another country. In the United

States, the law protects all citizens' rights. Citizens must respect the rules and laws in their society.

Punishments for breaking the law, like jail time, remind citizens to follow the laws.

Laws protect people. When people do not respect rules and laws, other people in the society might get hurt. If someone breaks a law, they might go to jail. Or they have to pay money to apologize for breaking the law. These punishments remind people to respect the laws of their society.

"Laws made by common consent must not be trampled on by individuals."
—President Thomas Jefferson

The Code of Ur-Nammu was written in a style called cuneiform.

CHAPTER TWO

RULES AND LAWS IN HISTORY

Rules and laws help to keep order within a civil society. Before people could write, laws were passed down through stories. After people learned to write, teaching the law became easier. People wrote laws in **legal codes**. In 2100 BCE, a country in a place called Mesopotamia created a legal code. It is called the Code of Ur-Nammu.

PRESIDENTS AND THE LAW

Citizens and leaders must respect laws. Even the president must follow laws. The US Constitution says if the president breaks the law, he can lose his job. This happened to President Richard Nixon in 1974.

Laws in Ancient Cultures

Ancient Greece had different sections called city-states. Each city-state had its own written laws. In Athens, Greece, citizens made decisions together. They also believed in equality under the law. Citizens respected and obeyed the laws they created.

Ancient Romans used the Twelve Tables (shown in this engraving) to understand their laws.

The ancient Romans shared the same ideas about citizens and laws as the ancient Greeks. However, the Romans also believed citizens had the right to have possessions. They thought all citizens should be protected and have civic values. They lived under shared rules and laws. These rules and laws were known as the Twelve Tables. This legal code helped other countries create rules.

> "No man is above the law and no man is below it ... Obedience to the law is demanded as a right; not asked as a favor." —President Theodore Roosevelt

In medieval England, kings did not have to follow laws. They created laws. They also made sure citizens followed laws. They punished people if they broke the law. Not everyone liked that the king had so

THE CODE OF UR-NAMMU

The Code of Ur-Nammu was written on tablets. It was written in a language called Sumerian. The code arranges laws in an IF (crime) THEN (punishment) format. This was one of the first times a code had been arranged this way. It shows how laws were created to bring order and gain respect.

In 1215, England's King John signed the Magna Carta.

much power. In 1215 CE, a group of lords rebelled against the English king John. They gave him a document that told the king his rights. It also said what the king could and couldn't do. This document was called the Magna Carta. It helped citizens have more equal rights.

Looking to the Magna Carta

In 1776, American **colonists** used the Magna Carta to explain why they wanted to be independent from England. After winning the American Revolution in 1783, America's Founding Fathers used the Magna Carta to help write the Constitution and the **Bill of Rights**.

The Bill of Rights protects citizens from unfair actions by the government.

CHRONOLOGY

2050 BCE Ur-Nammu's Code is written down on ancient tablets.

1760 BCE Hammurabi's Code becomes one of the first legal codes in an ancient society.

450 BCE The Twelve Tables are written and followed by ancient Romans.

1215 CE King John of England signs the Magna Carta.

1787 The Constitution of the United States of America is signed.

1791 The American Bill of Rights adds important laws to the US Constitution.

The Founding Fathers wrote the US Constitution. From left to right are: John Adams, Robert Morris, Alexander Hamilton, and Thomas Jefferson.

CHAPTER THREE

CONSTITUTIONAL RIGHTS: RESPECT FOR RULES AND LAWS

The Americans who wrote the US Constitution put a lot of thought and care into the document. One of the key parts of the US Constitution is respect for rules and laws. Why was respect for rules and laws important to America's Founding Fathers? Their own rights had been disrespected by the British.

Creating the Constitution

After gaining independence from England, America's founders drafted new rules and laws for the United States. These rules and laws were called the Articles of Confederation. All thirteen states agreed to follow them.

However, the Founders were afraid of giving the main government too much power. They agreed

In the 1700s, British soldiers (redcoats) disrespected the American colonists and treated them badly.

RULES AND LAWS IN THE CONSTITUTION

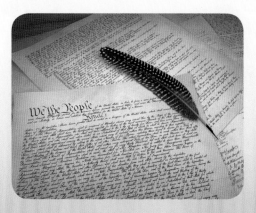

Today, many of the rules and laws in the US Constitution are the same rules and laws first written in 1787. This means that the rules and laws have worked for the country for hundreds of years. There have been some changes, though. These changes help make the Constitution better for today's society.

that the states could also have power. The states would work like separate countries. Many Americans liked this idea. However, not everyone was happy.

> "It is very important in a republic, that the people should respect the laws, for if we throw them to the winds, what becomes of civil government?" —Elizabeth Cady Stanton, social activist

Problems began. Congress made and passed laws, but they did not have the power to enforce these laws. Things needed to change.

The Constitutional Convention

In 1787, the Founders and other state representatives met at the Constitutional Convention in Philadelphia, Pennsylvania. They debated, argued, and finally agreed to write a document that everyone in the United States would follow. This became the Constitution. However, not everyone was happy with it. Certain citizens' rights were not thought about. In 1791, ten changes were added to the Constitution.

These changes became known as the Bill of Rights. The Bill of Rights and other amendments make sure every citizen has specific freedoms. The government must respect these freedoms.

Important Rights in the Constitution

The First Amendment protects freedom of religion, freedom of speech, freedom to assemble, and freedom of the press.

The US Constitution also guarantees a **social contract**. This means that if a person follows rules and laws, they will usually have a good life as a citizen.

The US Constitution was the first document that made the government respect and uphold its laws. It also was the first document to promise certain rights to its people.

American citizens
all have the right to
vote in elections.

CHAPTER FOUR

RESPECTING RULES AND LAWS TODAY

A merican citizens practice respect for rules and laws in a number of ways. First, they respect rules and laws by knowing and following them. If people know and follow rules and laws, they can be good citizens. Society runs smoothly and peacefully when everyone understands and respects the laws. Another way to respect rules and laws is by getting involved in society. Voting, helping others, and cleaning up local communities are ways to help

Sometimes, laws need to be challenged to make new laws. In the 1800s, many people were unhappy with slavery in the southern United States. People in the South could have slaves. Slaves worked on farms or in a person's house. In 1863, President Abraham Lincoln signed the Emancipation Proclamation. This document said everyone in the United States was free. A law called the Thirteenth Amendment also said people in the United States could no longer have slaves. The southern part of the country was at war during this time with the northern part. After the war, every state in the United States had to respect the Thirteenth Amendment. Slavery had ended.

society. If you follow the rules of caring for the

"The rule of law ... the foundation for all of our basic rights." —US Supreme Court Justice Sonia Sotomayor

world and each other, you will make the world a better place.

American citizens speak out to let leaders know when they have disrespected laws.

The First Amendment protects the most important US rights: the rights of its citizens. Americans show respect for this law. Sometimes they do this by speaking up when one of the First Amendment rights is in danger.

Ways to Get Involved

Today, leaders and government officials sometimes disrespect rules and laws. If that happens, citizens can look to the Constitution to let leaders and government officials know they are wrong. The Constitution protects citizens. It is important to respect the rules and laws in it. The Constitution makes sure everyone knows the rules and follows the rules. Some ways to get involved in your community if an official disrespects rules and laws include writing letters, calling government officials, and standing up for the rights of all citizens.

GLOSSARY

Bill of Rights The first ten amendments to the Constitution listing specific rights of citizens.

colonists People who lived in the United States when the United States was ruled by England.

constitution A document describing the system of beliefs and laws governing a country, state, or organization.

legal codes Laws written down and enforced by a city, state, or government.

order An arrangement of people in relation to each other according to a particular method.

rule of law An idea that states only the law should rule a nation.

social contract An agreement among people and their government that defines and limits the rights and duties of each.

society A group of people living together in a community.

FIND OUT MORE

Books

Hamilton, John. *How a Bill Becomes a Law.* Edina, MN:
ABDO Publishing, 2005.

Javernick, Ellen. *What If Everybody Did That?* New York:
Two Lions, 2012.

Website

The National Constitution Center

https://constitutioncenter.org/experience

Video

Schoolhouse Rock! "I'm Just a Bill"

https://vimeo.com/24334724

This animated music video shows how a bill becomes a law in
the US government.

INDEX

Page numbers in **boldface** are illustrations. Entries in **boldface** are glossary terms.

ABOUT THE AUTHOR

Elizabeth Schulz has been a writer her entire life, writing both professionally and for pleasure. In addition to writing for Cavendish Square Publishing, other writing credits include the WXXI PBS television series *New York Wine & Table* and story contributions for the daily historical podcast *On This Day*.